CAMPING JOURNAL

BELONGS TO:

_____

CAMPGROUND: _____

DATE: _____ SITE NO: _____

LOCATION: _____

_____

_____

WEATHER: _____ RATING: ☆ ☆ ☆ ☆ ☆

COMPANIONS: _____

_____

_____

PLACES VISITED: _____

_____

_____

_____

_____

ACTIVITIES: _____

_____

_____

_____

_____

PEOPLE MET: _____

_____

_____

TO DO NEXT TIME: _____

_____

_____

NOTES:

_____

_____

_____

_____

_____

_____

_____

_____

_____

_____

_____

_____

_____

PHOTO/DRAWING:

CAMPGROUND: _____

DATE: _____   SITE NO: _____

LOCATION: _____
_____
_____

WEATHER: _____   RATING: ☆ ☆ ☆ ☆ ☆

COMPANIONS: _____
_____
_____

PLACES VISITED: _____
_____
_____
_____
_____

ACTIVITIES: _____
_____
_____
_____
_____

PEOPLE MET: _____
_____
_____

TO DO NEXT TIME: _____
_____
_____

NOTES: _____

_____

_____

_____

_____

_____

_____

_____

_____

_____

_____

_____

PHOTO/DRAWING:

CAMPGROUND: _____

DATE: _____ SITE NO: _____

LOCATION: _____

_____

_____

WEATHER: _____ RATING: ☆ ☆ ☆ ☆ ☆

COMPANIONS: _____

_____

_____

PLACES VISITED: _____

_____

_____

_____

_____

ACTIVITIES: _____

_____

_____

_____

_____

_____

PEOPLE MET: _____

_____

_____

_____

TO DO NEXT TIME: _____

_____

_____

NOTES: _____

_____

_____

_____

_____

_____

_____

_____

_____

_____

_____

_____

PHOTO/DRAWING:

CAMPGROUND: _____

DATE: _____ SITE NO: _____

LOCATION: _____
_____
_____

WEATHER: _____ RATING: ☆ ☆ ☆ ☆ ☆

COMPANIONS: _____
_____
_____

PLACES VISITED: _____
_____
_____
_____
_____

ACTIVITIES: _____
_____
_____
_____
_____

PEOPLE MET: _____
_____
_____

TO DO NEXT TIME: _____
_____
_____

NOTES: _____

_____

_____

_____

_____

_____

_____

_____

_____

_____

_____

_____

_____

_____

PHOTO/DRAWING:

CAMPGROUND: _____

DATE: _____ SITE NO: _____

LOCATION: _____
_____
_____

WEATHER: _____ RATING: ☆ ☆ ☆ ☆ ☆

COMPANIONS: _____
_____
_____

PLACES VISITED: _____
_____
_____
_____
_____

ACTIVITIES: _____
_____
_____
_____
_____

PEOPLE MET: _____
_____
_____

TO DO NEXT TIME: _____
_____
_____

NOTES: _____

_____

_____

_____

_____

_____

_____

_____

_____

_____

_____

_____

_____

PHOTO/DRAWING:

CAMPGROUND: _____

DATE: _____ SITE NO: _____

LOCATION: _____
_____
_____

WEATHER: _____ RATING: ☆ ☆ ☆ ☆ ☆

COMPANIONS: _____
_____
_____

PLACES VISITED: _____
_____
_____
_____
_____

ACTIVITIES: _____
_____
_____
_____
_____

PEOPLE MET: _____
_____
_____

TO DO NEXT TIME: _____
_____
_____

NOTES: _____

_____

_____

_____

_____

_____

_____

_____

_____

_____

_____

_____

_____

PHOTO/DRAWING:

CAMPGROUND: _____

DATE: _____ SITE NO: _____

LOCATION: _____

_____

_____

WEATHER: _____ RATING: ☆ ☆ ☆ ☆ ☆

COMPANIONS: _____

_____

_____

PLACES VISITED: _____

_____

_____

_____

_____

ACTIVITIES: _____

_____

_____

_____

_____

PEOPLE MET: _____

_____

_____

TO DO NEXT TIME: _____

_____

_____

NOTES: _____

_____

_____

_____

_____

_____

_____

_____

_____

_____

_____

_____

_____

PHOTO/DRAWING:

CAMPGROUND: _____

DATE: _____   SITE NO: _____

LOCATION: _____

_____

_____

WEATHER: _____   RATING: ☆ ☆ ☆ ☆ ☆

COMPANIONS: _____

_____

_____

PLACES VISITED: _____

_____

_____

_____

_____

ACTIVITIES: _____

_____

_____

_____

_____

PEOPLE MET: _____

_____

_____

TO DO NEXT TIME: _____

_____

_____

NOTES: _____

_____

_____

_____

_____

_____

_____

_____

_____

_____

_____

_____

_____

PHOTO/DRAWING:

CAMPGROUND: _____

DATE: _____ SITE NO: _____

LOCATION: _____

_____

_____

WEATHER: _____ RATING: ☆ ☆ ☆ ☆ ☆

COMPANIONS: _____

_____

_____

PLACES VISITED: _____

_____

_____

_____

_____

ACTIVITIES: _____

_____

_____

_____

_____

PEOPLE MET: _____

_____

_____

TO DO NEXT TIME: _____

_____

_____

NOTES:

_____

_____

_____

_____

_____

_____

_____

_____

_____

_____

_____

_____

_____

_____

PHOTO/DRAWING:

CAMPGROUND: _____

DATE: _____   SITE NO: _____

LOCATION: _____

_____

_____

WEATHER: _____   RATING: ☆ ☆ ☆ ☆ ☆

COMPANIONS: _____

_____

_____

PLACES VISITED: _____

_____

_____

_____

_____

ACTIVITIES: _____

_____

_____

_____

_____

PEOPLE MET: _____

_____

_____

TO DO NEXT TIME: _____

_____

_____

NOTES: _____

_____

_____

_____

_____

_____

_____

_____

_____

_____

_____

_____

_____

PHOTO/DRAWING:

CAMPGROUND: _____

DATE: _____ SITE NO: _____

LOCATION: _____
_____
_____

WEATHER: _____ RATING: ☆ ☆ ☆ ☆ ☆

COMPANIONS: _____
_____
_____

PLACES VISITED: _____
_____
_____
_____
_____

ACTIVITIES: _____
_____
_____
_____
_____

PEOPLE MET: _____
_____
_____

TO DO NEXT TIME: _____
_____
_____

NOTES: _____

_____

_____

_____

_____

_____

_____

_____

_____

_____

_____

_____

PHOTO/DRAWING:

CAMPGROUND: _____

DATE: _____ SITE NO: _____

LOCATION: _____

_____

_____

WEATHER: _____ RATING: ☆ ☆ ☆ ☆ ☆

COMPANIONS: _____

_____

_____

PLACES VISITED: _____

_____

_____

_____

_____

ACTIVITIES: _____

_____

_____

_____

_____

PEOPLE MET: _____

_____

_____

TO DO NEXT TIME: _____

_____

_____

NOTES:

_____

_____

_____

_____

_____

_____

_____

_____

_____

_____

_____

_____

_____

_____

_____

_____

PHOTO/DRAWING:

CAMPGROUND: _____

DATE: _____ SITE NO: _____

LOCATION: _____
_____
_____

WEATHER: _____ RATING: ☆ ☆ ☆ ☆ ☆

COMPANIONS: _____
_____
_____

PLACES VISITED: _____
_____
_____
_____
_____
_____

ACTIVITIES: _____
_____
_____
_____
_____
_____

PEOPLE MET: _____
_____
_____
_____

TO DO NEXT TIME: _____
_____
_____

NOTES: _____

_____

_____

_____

_____

_____

_____

_____

_____

_____

_____

_____

PHOTO/DRAWING:

CAMPGROUND: _____

DATE: _____ SITE NO: _____

LOCATION: _____
_____
_____

WEATHER: _____ RATING: ☆ ☆ ☆ ☆ ☆

COMPANIONS: _____
_____
_____

PLACES VISITED: _____
_____
_____
_____
_____

ACTIVITIES: _____
_____
_____
_____
_____

PEOPLE MET: _____
_____
_____

TO DO NEXT TIME: _____
_____
_____

NOTES:

_____

_____

_____

_____

_____

_____

_____

_____

_____

_____

_____

_____

PHOTO/DRAWING:

CAMPGROUND: _____

DATE: _____ SITE NO: _____

LOCATION: _____

_____

_____

WEATHER: _____ RATING: ☆ ☆ ☆ ☆ ☆

COMPANIONS: _____

_____

_____

PLACES VISITED: _____

_____

_____

_____

_____

ACTIVITIES: _____

_____

_____

_____

_____

PEOPLE MET: _____

_____

_____

TO DO NEXT TIME: _____

_____

_____

NOTES: _____

_____
_____
_____
_____
_____
_____
_____
_____
_____
_____
_____

PHOTO/DRAWING:

CAMPGROUND: _____

DATE: _____ SITE NO: _____

LOCATION: _____

_____

_____

WEATHER: _____ RATING: ☆ ☆ ☆ ☆ ☆

COMPANIONS: _____

_____

_____

PLACES VISITED: _____

_____

_____

_____

_____

ACTIVITIES: _____

_____

_____

_____

_____

PEOPLE MET: _____

_____

_____

TO DO NEXT TIME: _____

_____

_____

NOTES: _____

_____
_____
_____
_____
_____
_____
_____
_____
_____
_____
_____
_____
_____

PHOTO/DRAWING:

CAMPGROUND: _____

DATE: _____ SITE NO: _____

LOCATION: _____

_____

_____

WEATHER: _____ RATING: ☆ ☆ ☆ ☆ ☆

COMPANIONS: _____

_____

_____

PLACES VISITED: _____

_____

_____

_____

_____

ACTIVITIES: _____

_____

_____

_____

_____

PEOPLE MET: _____

_____

_____

TO DO NEXT TIME: _____

_____

_____

NOTES:

_____

_____

_____

_____

_____

_____

_____

_____

_____

_____

_____

_____

_____

PHOTO/DRAWING:

CAMPGROUND: _____

DATE: _____ SITE NO: _____

LOCATION: _____

_____

_____

WEATHER: _____ RATING: ☆ ☆ ☆ ☆ ☆

COMPANIONS: _____

_____

_____

PLACES VISITED: _____

_____

_____

_____

_____

ACTIVITIES: _____

_____

_____

_____

_____

PEOPLE MET: _____

_____

_____

TO DO NEXT TIME: _____

_____

_____

NOTES: _____

_____

_____

_____

_____

_____

_____

_____

_____

_____

_____

_____

_____

_____

PHOTO/DRAWING:

CAMPGROUND: _____

DATE: _____ SITE NO: _____

LOCATION: _____

_____

_____

WEATHER: _____ RATING: ☆ ☆ ☆ ☆ ☆

COMPANIONS: _____

_____

_____

PLACES VISITED: _____

_____

_____

_____

_____

ACTIVITIES: _____

_____

_____

_____

_____

PEOPLE MET: _____

_____

_____

TO DO NEXT TIME: _____

_____

_____

NOTES:

_____

_____

_____

_____

_____

_____

_____

_____

_____

_____

_____

_____

PHOTO/DRAWING:

CAMPGROUND: _____

DATE: _____ SITE NO: _____

LOCATION: _____

_____

_____

WEATHER: _____ RATING: ☆ ☆ ☆ ☆ ☆

COMPANIONS: _____

_____

_____

PLACES VISITED: _____

_____

_____

_____

_____

ACTIVITIES: _____

_____

_____

_____

_____

PEOPLE MET: _____

_____

_____

TO DO NEXT TIME: _____

_____

_____

NOTES: _____

_____

_____

_____

_____

_____

_____

_____

_____

_____

_____

_____

_____

PHOTO/DRAWING:

CAMPGROUND: _____

DATE: _____ SITE NO: _____

LOCATION: _____

_____

_____

WEATHER: _____ RATING: ☆ ☆ ☆ ☆ ☆

COMPANIONS: _____

_____

_____

PLACES VISITED: _____

_____

_____

_____

_____

ACTIVITIES: _____

_____

_____

_____

_____

PEOPLE MET: _____

_____

_____

TO DO NEXT TIME: _____

_____

_____

NOTES: _____

_____

_____

_____

_____

_____

_____

_____

_____

_____

_____

_____

_____

PHOTO/DRAWING:

CAMPGROUND: _____

DATE: _____ SITE NO: _____

LOCATION: _____

_____

_____

WEATHER: _____ RATING: ☆ ☆ ☆ ☆ ☆

COMPANIONS: _____

_____

_____

PLACES VISITED: _____

_____

_____

_____

_____

ACTIVITIES: _____

_____

_____

_____

_____

PEOPLE MET: _____

_____

_____

TO DO NEXT TIME: _____

_____

_____

NOTES: _____

_____
_____
_____
_____
_____
_____
_____
_____
_____
_____
_____
_____
_____

PHOTO/DRAWING:

CAMPGROUND: _____

DATE: _____   SITE NO: _____

LOCATION: _____

_____

_____

WEATHER: _____   RATING: ☆ ☆ ☆ ☆ ☆

COMPANIONS: _____

_____

_____

PLACES VISITED: _____

_____

_____

_____

_____

ACTIVITIES: _____

_____

_____

_____

_____

PEOPLE MET: _____

_____

_____

TO DO NEXT TIME: _____

_____

_____

NOTES:

_____

_____

_____

_____

_____

_____

_____

_____

_____

_____

_____

_____

PHOTO/DRAWING:

CAMPGROUND: _____

DATE: _____ SITE NO: _____

LOCATION: _____

_____

_____

WEATHER: _____ RATING: ☆ ☆ ☆ ☆ ☆

COMPANIONS: _____

_____

_____

PLACES VISITED: _____

_____

_____

_____

_____

ACTIVITIES: _____

_____

_____

_____

_____

PEOPLE MET: _____

_____

_____

TO DO NEXT TIME: _____

_____

_____

NOTES:

_____

_____

_____

_____

_____

_____

_____

_____

_____

_____

_____

_____

_____

PHOTO/DRAWING:

CAMPGROUND: _____

DATE: _____ SITE NO: _____

LOCATION: _____

_____

_____

WEATHER: _____ RATING: ☆ ☆ ☆ ☆ ☆

COMPANIONS: _____

_____

_____

PLACES VISITED: _____

_____

_____

_____

_____

_____

ACTIVITIES: _____

_____

_____

_____

_____

_____

PEOPLE MET: _____

_____

_____

TO DO NEXT TIME: _____

_____

_____

NOTES: _____

_____

_____

_____

_____

_____

_____

_____

_____

_____

_____

_____

PHOTO/DRAWING:

CAMPGROUND: _____

DATE: _____ SITE NO: _____

LOCATION: _____

_____

_____

WEATHER: _____ RATING: ☆ ☆ ☆ ☆ ☆

COMPANIONS: _____

_____

_____

PLACES VISITED: _____

_____

_____

_____

_____

ACTIVITIES: _____

_____

_____

_____

_____

PEOPLE MET: _____

_____

_____

TO DO NEXT TIME: _____

_____

_____

NOTES: _____

_____

_____

_____

_____

_____

_____

_____

_____

_____

_____

_____

PHOTO/DRAWING:

CAMPGROUND: _____

DATE: _____ SITE NO: _____

LOCATION: _____

_____

_____

WEATHER: _____ RATING: ☆ ☆ ☆ ☆ ☆

COMPANIONS: _____

_____

_____

PLACES VISITED: _____

_____

_____

_____

_____

ACTIVITIES: _____

_____

_____

_____

_____

PEOPLE MET: _____

_____

_____

TO DO NEXT TIME: _____

_____

_____

NOTES: _____

_____

_____

_____

_____

_____

_____

_____

_____

_____

_____

_____

PHOTO/DRAWING:

CAMPGROUND: _____

DATE: _____ SITE NO: _____

LOCATION: _____

_____

_____

WEATHER: _____ RATING: ☆ ☆ ☆ ☆ ☆

COMPANIONS: _____

_____

_____

PLACES VISITED: _____

_____

_____

_____

_____

ACTIVITIES: _____

_____

_____

_____

_____

PEOPLE MET: _____

_____

_____

TO DO NEXT TIME: _____

_____

_____

NOTES:

_____

_____

_____

_____

_____

_____

_____

_____

_____

_____

_____

_____

PHOTO/DRAWING:

CAMPGROUND: _____

DATE: _____ SITE NO: _____

LOCATION: _____

_____

_____

WEATHER: _____ RATING: ☆ ☆ ☆ ☆ ☆

COMPANIONS: _____

_____

_____

PLACES VISITED: _____

_____

_____

_____

_____

ACTIVITIES: _____

_____

_____

_____

_____

PEOPLE MET: _____

_____

_____

TO DO NEXT TIME: _____

_____

_____

NOTES:

_____

_____

_____

_____

_____

_____

_____

_____

_____

_____

_____

_____

PHOTO/DRAWING:

CAMPGROUND: _____

DATE: _____ SITE NO: _____

LOCATION: _____

_____

_____

WEATHER: _____ RATING: ☆ ☆ ☆ ☆ ☆

COMPANIONS: _____

_____

_____

PLACES VISITED: _____

_____

_____

_____

_____

_____

ACTIVITIES: _____

_____

_____

_____

_____

_____

PEOPLE MET: _____

_____

_____

_____

TO DO NEXT TIME: _____

_____

_____

_____

NOTES:

_____

_____

_____

_____

_____

_____

_____

_____

_____

_____

_____

_____

_____

PHOTO/DRAWING:

CAMPGROUND: _____

DATE: _____ SITE NO: _____

LOCATION: _____

_____

_____

WEATHER: _____ RATING: ☆ ☆ ☆ ☆ ☆

COMPANIONS: _____

_____

_____

PLACES VISITED: _____

_____

_____

_____

_____

ACTIVITIES: _____

_____

_____

_____

_____

PEOPLE MET: _____

_____

_____

TO DO NEXT TIME: _____

_____

_____

NOTES:

_____

_____

_____

_____

_____

_____

_____

_____

_____

_____

_____

_____

PHOTO/DRAWING:

CAMPGROUND: _____

DATE: _____ SITE NO: _____

LOCATION: _____

_____

_____

WEATHER: _____ RATING: ☆ ☆ ☆ ☆ ☆

COMPANIONS: _____

_____

_____

PLACES VISITED: _____

_____

_____

_____

_____

ACTIVITIES: _____

_____

_____

_____

_____

PEOPLE MET: _____

_____

_____

TO DO NEXT TIME: _____

_____

_____

NOTES: _____

_____

_____

_____

_____

_____

_____

_____

_____

_____

_____

_____

_____

PHOTO/DRAWING:

CAMPGROUND: _____

DATE: _____ SITE NO: _____

LOCATION: _____
_____
_____

WEATHER: _____ RATING: ☆ ☆ ☆ ☆ ☆

COMPANIONS: _____
_____
_____

PLACES VISITED: _____
_____
_____
_____
_____

ACTIVITIES: _____
_____
_____
_____
_____

PEOPLE MET: _____
_____
_____

TO DO NEXT TIME: _____
_____
_____

NOTES: _____
_____
_____
_____
_____
_____
_____
_____
_____
_____
_____
_____
_____

PHOTO/DRAWING:

CAMPGROUND: _____

DATE: _____   SITE NO: _____

LOCATION: _____

_____

_____

WEATHER: _____   RATING: ☆ ☆ ☆ ☆ ☆

COMPANIONS: _____

_____

_____

PLACES VISITED: _____

_____

_____

_____

_____

_____

ACTIVITIES: _____

_____

_____

_____

_____

_____

PEOPLE MET: _____

_____

_____

_____

TO DO NEXT TIME: _____

_____

_____

NOTES: _____

_____

_____

_____

_____

_____

_____

_____

_____

_____

_____

_____

_____

PHOTO/DRAWING:

CAMPGROUND: _____

DATE: _____ SITE NO: _____

LOCATION: _____

_____

_____

WEATHER: _____ RATING: ☆ ☆ ☆ ☆ ☆

COMPANIONS: _____

_____

_____

PLACES VISITED: _____

_____

_____

_____

_____

ACTIVITIES: _____

_____

_____

_____

_____

PEOPLE MET: _____

_____

_____

TO DO NEXT TIME: _____

_____

_____

NOTES: _____

_____

_____

_____

_____

_____

_____

_____

_____

_____

_____

_____

_____

PHOTO/DRAWING:

CAMPGROUND: _____

DATE: _____ SITE NO: _____

LOCATION: _____

_____

_____

WEATHER: _____ RATING: ☆ ☆ ☆ ☆ ☆

COMPANIONS: _____

_____

_____

PLACES VISITED: _____

_____

_____

_____

_____

ACTIVITIES: _____

_____

_____

_____

_____

PEOPLE MET: _____

_____

_____

TO DO NEXT TIME: _____

_____

_____

NOTES: _____

_____

_____

_____

_____

_____

_____

_____

_____

_____

_____

_____

_____

_____

_____

PHOTO/DRAWING:

CAMPGROUND: _____

DATE: _____   SITE NO: _____

LOCATION: _____

_____

_____

WEATHER: _____   RATING: ☆ ☆ ☆ ☆ ☆

COMPANIONS: _____

_____

_____

PLACES VISITED: _____

_____

_____

_____

_____

ACTIVITIES: _____

_____

_____

_____

_____

PEOPLE MET: _____

_____

_____

TO DO NEXT TIME: _____

_____

_____

NOTES: _____

_____

_____

_____

_____

_____

_____

_____

_____

_____

_____

_____

PHOTO/DRAWING:

CAMPGROUND: _____

DATE: _____ SITE NO: _____

LOCATION: _____
_____
_____

WEATHER: _____ RATING: ☆ ☆ ☆ ☆ ☆

COMPANIONS: _____
_____
_____

PLACES VISITED: _____
_____
_____
_____
_____

ACTIVITIES: _____
_____
_____
_____
_____

PEOPLE MET: _____
_____
_____

TO DO NEXT TIME: _____
_____
_____

NOTES:

_____

_____

_____

_____

_____

_____

_____

_____

_____

_____

_____

_____

_____

PHOTO/DRAWING:

CAMPGROUND: _____

DATE: _____ SITE NO: _____

LOCATION: _____

_____

_____

WEATHER: _____ RATING: ☆ ☆ ☆ ☆ ☆

COMPANIONS: _____

_____

_____

PLACES VISITED: _____

_____

_____

_____

_____

ACTIVITIES: _____

_____

_____

_____

_____

PEOPLE MET: _____

_____

_____

TO DO NEXT TIME: _____

_____

_____

NOTES: _____

_____

_____

_____

_____

_____

_____

_____

_____

_____

_____

_____

_____

PHOTO/DRAWING:

CAMPGROUND: _____

DATE: _____ SITE NO: _____

LOCATION: _____
_____
_____

WEATHER: _____ RATING: ☆ ☆ ☆ ☆ ☆

COMPANIONS: _____
_____
_____

PLACES VISITED: _____
_____
_____
_____
_____

ACTIVITIES: _____
_____
_____
_____
_____

PEOPLE MET: _____
_____
_____

TO DO NEXT TIME: _____
_____
_____

NOTES: _____

_____

_____

_____

_____

_____

_____

_____

_____

_____

_____

_____

_____

PHOTO/DRAWING:

CAMPGROUND: _____

DATE: _____ SITE NO: _____

LOCATION: _____
_____
_____

WEATHER: _____ RATING: ☆ ☆ ☆ ☆ ☆

COMPANIONS: _____
_____
_____

PLACES VISITED: _____
_____
_____
_____
_____

ACTIVITIES: _____
_____
_____
_____
_____

PEOPLE MET: _____
_____
_____

TO DO NEXT TIME: _____
_____
_____

NOTES: _____

_____

_____

_____

_____

_____

_____

_____

_____

_____

_____

_____

_____

PHOTO/DRAWING:

CAMPGROUND: _____

DATE: _____   SITE NO: _____

LOCATION: _____

_____

_____

WEATHER: _____   RATING: ☆ ☆ ☆ ☆ ☆

COMPANIONS: _____

_____

_____

PLACES VISITED: _____

_____

_____

_____

_____

ACTIVITIES: _____

_____

_____

_____

_____

PEOPLE MET: _____

_____

_____

TO DO NEXT TIME: _____

_____

_____

NOTES: _____

_____

_____

_____

_____

_____

_____

_____

_____

_____

PHOTO/DRAWING:

CAMPGROUND: _____

DATE: _____ SITE NO: _____

LOCATION: _____
_____
_____

WEATHER: _____ RATING: ☆ ☆ ☆ ☆ ☆

COMPANIONS: _____
_____
_____

PLACES VISITED: _____
_____
_____
_____
_____

ACTIVITIES: _____
_____
_____
_____
_____

PEOPLE MET: _____
_____
_____

TO DO NEXT TIME: _____
_____
_____

NOTES: _____

_____

_____

_____

_____

_____

_____

_____

_____

_____

_____

_____

_____

PHOTO/DRAWING:

CAMPGROUND: _____

DATE: _____ SITE NO: _____

LOCATION: _____
_____
_____

WEATHER: _____ RATING: ☆ ☆ ☆ ☆ ☆

COMPANIONS: _____
_____
_____

PLACES VISITED: _____
_____
_____
_____
_____

ACTIVITIES: _____
_____
_____
_____
_____

PEOPLE MET: _____
_____
_____

TO DO NEXT TIME: _____
_____
_____

NOTES: _____

_____

_____

_____

_____

_____

_____

_____

_____

_____

_____

PHOTO/DRAWING:

CAMPGROUND: _____

DATE: _____ SITE NO: _____

LOCATION: _____

_____

_____

WEATHER: _____ RATING: ☆ ☆ ☆ ☆ ☆

COMPANIONS: _____

_____

_____

PLACES VISITED: _____

_____

_____

_____

_____

ACTIVITIES: _____

_____

_____

_____

_____

PEOPLE MET: _____

_____

_____

_____

TO DO NEXT TIME: _____

_____

_____

_____

NOTES: _____

_____

_____

_____

_____

_____

_____

_____

_____

_____

_____

PHOTO/DRAWING:

CAMPGROUND: _____

DATE: _____ SITE NO: _____

LOCATION: _____

_____

_____

WEATHER: _____ RATING: ☆ ☆ ☆ ☆ ☆

COMPANIONS: _____

_____

_____

PLACES VISITED: _____

_____

_____

_____

_____

ACTIVITIES: _____

_____

_____

_____

_____

PEOPLE MET: _____

_____

_____

TO DO NEXT TIME: _____

_____

_____

NOTES: _____
_____
_____
_____
_____
_____
_____
_____
_____
_____
_____
_____

PHOTO/DRAWING:

CAMPGROUND: _____

DATE: _____ SITE NO: _____

LOCATION: _____

_____

_____

WEATHER: _____ RATING: ☆ ☆ ☆ ☆ ☆

COMPANIONS: _____

_____

_____

PLACES VISITED: _____

_____

_____

_____

_____

ACTIVITIES: _____

_____

_____

_____

_____

PEOPLE MET: _____

_____

_____

TO DO NEXT TIME: _____

_____

_____

NOTES: _____

_____

_____

_____

_____

_____

_____

_____

_____

_____

_____

_____

_____

_____

PHOTO/DRAWING:

CAMPGROUND: _____

DATE: _____ SITE NO: _____

LOCATION: _____

_____

_____

WEATHER: _____ RATING: ☆ ☆ ☆ ☆ ☆

COMPANIONS: _____

_____

_____

PLACES VISITED: _____

_____

_____

_____

_____

ACTIVITIES: _____

_____

_____

_____

_____

PEOPLE MET: _____

_____

_____

TO DO NEXT TIME: _____

_____

_____

NOTES: _____

_____

_____

_____

_____

_____

_____

_____

_____

_____

_____

PHOTO/DRAWING:

CAMPGROUND: _____

DATE: _____ SITE NO: _____

LOCATION: _____

_____

_____

WEATHER: _____ RATING: ☆ ☆ ☆ ☆ ☆

COMPANIONS: _____

_____

_____

PLACES VISITED: _____

_____

_____

_____

_____

ACTIVITIES: _____

_____

_____

_____

_____

PEOPLE MET: _____

_____

_____

TO DO NEXT TIME: _____

_____

_____

NOTES:

_____

_____

_____

_____

_____

_____

_____

_____

_____

_____

_____

_____

PHOTO/DRAWING:

CAMPGROUND: _____

DATE: _____ SITE NO: _____

LOCATION: _____

_____

_____

WEATHER: _____ RATING: ☆ ☆ ☆ ☆ ☆

COMPANIONS: _____

_____

_____

PLACES VISITED: _____

_____

_____

_____

_____

ACTIVITIES: _____

_____

_____

_____

_____

PEOPLE MET: _____

_____

_____

TO DO NEXT TIME: _____

_____

_____

NOTES: _____
_____
_____
_____
_____
_____
_____
_____
_____
_____
_____
_____
_____
_____

PHOTO/DRAWING:

CAMPGROUND: _____

DATE: _____ SITE NO: _____

LOCATION: _____

_____

_____

WEATHER: _____ RATING: ☆ ☆ ☆ ☆ ☆

COMPANIONS: _____

_____

_____

PLACES VISITED: _____

_____

_____

_____

_____

ACTIVITIES: _____

_____

_____

_____

_____

PEOPLE MET: _____

_____

_____

TO DO NEXT TIME: _____

_____

_____

NOTES: _____

_____

_____

_____

_____

_____

_____

_____

_____

_____

_____

_____

_____

PHOTO/DRAWING:

CAMPGROUND: _____

DATE: _____ SITE NO: _____

LOCATION: _____

_____

_____

WEATHER: _____ RATING: ☆ ☆ ☆ ☆ ☆

COMPANIONS: _____

_____

_____

PLACES VISITED: _____

_____

_____

_____

_____

ACTIVITIES: _____

_____

_____

_____

_____

PEOPLE MET: _____

_____

_____

TO DO NEXT TIME: _____

_____

_____

_____

NOTES: _____

_____

_____

_____

_____

_____

_____

_____

_____

_____

_____

_____

_____

_____

PHOTO/DRAWING:

CAMPGROUND: _____

DATE: _____ SITE NO: _____

LOCATION: _____

_____

_____

WEATHER: _____ RATING: ☆ ☆ ☆ ☆ ☆

COMPANIONS: _____

_____

_____

PLACES VISITED: _____

_____

_____

_____

_____

ACTIVITIES: _____

_____

_____

_____

_____

PEOPLE MET: _____

_____

_____

TO DO NEXT TIME: _____

_____

_____

NOTES: _____

_____

_____

_____

_____

_____

_____

_____

_____

_____

_____

_____

_____

PHOTO/DRAWING:

CAMPGROUND: _____

DATE: _____   SITE NO: _____

LOCATION: _____

_____

_____

WEATHER: _____   RATING: ☆ ☆ ☆ ☆ ☆

COMPANIONS: _____

_____

_____

PLACES VISITED: _____

_____

_____

_____

_____

ACTIVITIES: _____

_____

_____

_____

_____

PEOPLE MET: _____

_____

_____

TO DO NEXT TIME: _____

_____

_____

NOTES: _____

_____

_____

_____

_____

_____

_____

_____

_____

_____

_____

PHOTO/DRAWING:

CAMPGROUND: _____

DATE: _____ SITE NO: _____

LOCATION: _____

_____

_____

WEATHER: _____ RATING: ☆ ☆ ☆ ☆ ☆

COMPANIONS: _____

_____

_____

PLACES VISITED: _____

_____

_____

_____

_____

_____

ACTIVITIES: _____

_____

_____

_____

_____

_____

PEOPLE MET: _____

_____

_____

_____

TO DO NEXT TIME: _____

_____

_____

NOTES: _____

_____

_____

_____

_____

_____

_____

_____

_____

_____

_____

_____

PHOTO/DRAWING:

Printed in Great Britain
by Amazon

44652682R00064